The Great Comforter

The Great Comforter

Adebisi Awonuga

WORDLINES EXTENSIONS

ISBN: 978-978-983-151-7

Unless otherwise stated, Scripture quotations are taken from the HOLY BIBLE, New King James Version, Copyright by Thomas Nelson Inc.

Scripture quotations marked NIV are taken from the HOLY BIBLE, New International Version, Copyright 1973, 1978, 1984 by International Bible Society.

Published by:
Wordlines Extensions,
24 Dupe Ogundimu Street,
Off Akeredolu Street,
Elebu,
Ibadan, Nigeria.
Tel: 08023246560

Cover design by KFI Expressionists

DEDICATION

This book is dedicated to all widows, widowers, the lonely, the deserted, those hurting and all those facing devastation.

TABLE OF CONTENTS

FOREWORD

I have known Mrs. Adebisi Awonuga as a friend, sister, prayer partner and confidante for over thirty-five (35) years. Bisi is indisputably a virtuous Christian woman of impeccable character and great repute. I have personally observed and admired her unwavering commitment to the Lord particularly as she walked through her difficult journey, enduring various challenging phases of life as shared in this book.

This book is a must read for those who yearn for encouragement and inspiration to take the transitional step from a place of pain to a joyful season of new beginnings. It is a spiritual treasure trove of truth, transparency and real-life struggles experienced by an uncompromising woman determined to follow the Lord's leading and plan for her life.

Her story is written to share the faithfulness and providence of God to His children. This book is replete with spiritual tools that are required to experience and enjoy the comfort and strengthening needed to confront the unavoidable challenging seasons of life.

My prayer is that this book's readership will span the four corners of this earth and be a true and worthy testament to the redeeming work of our Lord Jesus Christ in the lives of His precious children.

Nike Adeoye-Ladapo
Dallas, Texas, U.S.A.

ACKNOWLEDGEMENTS

"I will sing of the mercies of The Lord forever; with my mouth will I make known Thy faithfulness to all generations" (Psalm 89:1).

I give all glory, honour and adoration to my Lord God Almighty, The Eternal Rock of Ages, the Eternal King of Glory, my Lord and Saviour Jesus Christ, the Holy Spirit, the Great Comforter; for His abundant grace upon me through the changing scenes of life.

I thank and appreciate my darling husband, Emmanuel Oluwarotimi Awonuga who amongst others, encouraged me to continue to write this book, and for his usual understanding and humility.

I bless the Lord for my loving children, Oluwafeyikunmi and Oluwafakinkunmi who devoted some time to edit this book, and for all my other children too. They have all been wonderful, surrounding me with much love. May God bless them all in Jesus' name.

I thank my siblings and their families, my aunts, uncles, cousins and in-laws for being very caring, especially my eldest sister, Mrs. Olufunmilola Onanuga.

I also owe my gratitude to my long-time friend turned sister and prayer partner, Mrs. Nike Ladapo for graciously accepting to review this book, coupled with her excellent proofreading. I feel more honoured than deserved by her encomiums.

My special thanks to my friends more like sisters, Mrs. Anike Agbeja and Mrs. Ruth Idris for staying with me and standing by me during my trials and ups and downs of life. I also thank Kemi Ashomuyide who has been present from the beginning of the story.

My deep appreciation to Ebenezer Akin Olamilokun and his dear wife, Ronke Olamilokun; to Tolu Soyomokun and Dr. and Mrs. Babatunde Dinyo, for their consistent care and for being there for us all these years.

I also owe a debt of gratitude to ministers and members of The African Church, Elder and Mrs. Sete Aiyede and the entire members of Aiyede House Fellowship; Comforter's Companions Fellowship; Peace House Fellowship and of course my TACEF (The African Church Evangelical Fellowship) family.

I would also like to acknowledge my friend turned sister and mentor, Mrs. Folasade Adetiba, Mr. Aderibigbe Omole and Dr. Kole Abayomi SAN—all

of blessed memory.

I thank my first family friends in France, Jacques & Yvette Medjo who provided some of the flower photos in this book, and a host of other people who God has been using to surround me in this journey of life.

Adebisi Awonuga

Chapter One

INTRODUCTION

A week before I was widowed, I read in the "Daily Bread," a Christian daily devotional which I have been using for many years, about three life stories of people who at one time or the other were bereaved. Each of them did something positive about their grief: they encouraged other people in similar situations.

Little did I know then that God was preparing me to face what was about to happen. After I was widowed in 2003, I had a strong nudge to write this book and to set up a fellowship for widows and others in distress. While the fellowship, COMFORTER'S COMPANIONS FELLOWSHIP was founded in 2008, I relented in writing the book. Having read some books written by widows, I thought to myself that it was no longer necessary to add mine to the list.

I shared my thoughts with my friend Mrs. Ruth Idris, an evangelist. She disagreed with me and encouraged me to still write, possibly my readers would be different from those of other authors. I started writing but something in me kept on saying that I should wait a bit because there would be more testimonies to share.

I started writing again a few months afterwards, willing to share my testimony to encourage widows in particular and other people facing challenges, and to confirm that indeed the Holy Spirit is the Great Comforter. Our Lord Jesus Christ says in John 14:16-17, "And I will pray the Father, and He will give you another Helper, that He may abide with you forever—the Spirit of truth, whom the world cannot receive, because it neither sees Him nor knows Him; but you know Him, for He dwells with you and will be in you."

We are also to comfort others with the same comfort that we have received; as admonished in 2 Corinthians 1:3-4: "Blessed be the God and Father of our Lord Jesus Christ, the Father of mercies and God

of all comfort, who comforts us in all our tribulation, that we may be able to comfort those who are in any trouble, with the comfort with which we ourselves are comforted by God."

Chapter Two

GROWING IN HIS LOVE

A bouncing baby girl was born on a Saturday in December, in a yellow bungalow at Patey Street, Ebute-Meta, Lagos, Nigeria, to Mr. Joseph Adekunle Odedina and Mrs. Alice Alaba Olayiwola Odedina both of blessed memory. A happy couple that managed their electronics business well, had their challenges, but their faith, doggedness and resilience saw them through. They were God-fearing, contented people who maintained discipline and raised their children in the admonition of the Lord.

The baby, being the fifth child of her parents, coming after the loss of the fourth child, was given only two special names (unlike all the other children who have about four names): "Adebisi" meaning crown is fruitful, and "Oluwaremilekun" which literally means God has stopped my tears. At my baptism by immersion, I took up an additional name "Oluwasoromidayo" meaning, God has turned my matter to joy.

Our parents were very caring and loving. They paid our school fees promptly and were always there for us. I remember that Dad was the chairman of the PTA (Parents Teachers Association) in all our schools, and Mum was a virtuous woman in all ramifications. We were brought up to attend morning and evening services in church; also, morning and evening family devotions were compulsory. Raising us up in the fear and admonition of the Lord was of paramount importance to them.

SCHOOL DAYS

I started kindergarten at the age of four at Sisi Obasa Day Nursery School at Lady–Lak, Yaba, Lagos. At the age of six when my right hand could touch the tip of my left ear—that was the precondition for enrolment into elementary school in Nigeria in those days—I started primary school at Anglican Girls Primary School, Surulere, Lagos, a Christian missionary

school. Thereafter, I proceeded to Abeokuta Girls Grammar School, but was there for two years only, because I fell ill frequently. I had to change school, so I came back to Lagos and completed my secondary education at Lagos Anglican Girls Grammar School.

While at school, I loved march past. I often marched in front of my school sport's house flag during Inter–House Sports. It was the custom then for a school to invite students from other schools to her Inter–House Sports. It was on such occasion that one of my school friends, Yinka Max-Lino and I bumped into two young guys from Methodist Boys High School, Lagos. Yinka was a neighbour to one of them, named Richard Feyi Soyombo, now of blessed memory. The other guy attended the same church as I but I did not know his name. We just greeted each other and left.

Later in the week, Yinka informed me at school that the guy said he knew me in church, and would like to invite me to a luncheon the following Saturday. She said she would also be at the party.

In my home, late parties were not allowed, but being a luncheon, I sought my parents' permission to go because no child went out without permission. It was at that luncheon that the second guy and I became friends. Soon after, he became my first boyfriend.

I had my higher school education at the Comprehensive High School, Ayetoro and also did Cambridge International Baccalaureate A-Levels at Ogun State Polytechnic, as it was then called. Thereafter, I proceeded to study law as one of the pioneer Law students at the University of Ibadan, the premier university in Nigeria.

After graduating from the university, I studied at the Nigerian Law School, Victoria Island, Lagos. There I was called to the Bar in 1985 as Barrister and Solicitor of the Supreme Court of Nigeria. I was posted to Kaduna for the National Youth Service Corps.

CHRISTIAN ACTIVITIES

Being born into a Christian family, I was baptised as a child at The African Bethlehem Church, Ebute Meta with Mrs. Williams and Mrs. Winifred Ibidunni—both of blessed memory—as my god-mothers. Both of them were faithful and up to the task. Whilst Mrs. Williams, being a pastor's wife, saw to my spiritual upbringing; Mrs. Ibidunni, being a teacher at St Jude's school, saw to my excellent performance throughout my elementary education.

My parents later took us to The Apostolic Church where we worshipped for some years and eventually returned to The African Church.

They taught us to pray both in pleasant and difficult situations. I remember one accident that almost took my life and that of my sister, Folake. We were both travelling to our hometown, Abeokuta in my father's new Toyota Crown car driven by one of his favourite drivers, to join our parents. My other siblings had set out earlier along with our parents for one of my grand aunt's funeral. We set out comfortably well and the driver drove at reasonable speed on the old Abeokuta road. There was an

ongoing construction at that time. Somewhere along the road, there was a diversion. At that point, there was a man designated to direct traffic using signposts to instruct commuters on either side to go or stop, in order to prevent collision of vehicles.

For no just cause except distraction, the man suddenly changed the sign from 'go' to 'stop'. That made our driver apply the brakes abruptly, causing the car to lose control and somersault three times into the nearby bush. It was mercy a big tree stopped it, for behind the big tree was a stream.

As the car tumbled, I was just praying, "Lord Jesus, please save us." When the car finally stopped, the doors were damaged and could not be opened. The windows and windscreen had shattered. The only way to come out of the car was through the broken windows which gave some slight cuts on my hand; but apart from that, the three of us survived without any injury. Glory be to God Almighty!

Immediately after I got out of the car, I started running without really knowing why or where I was running to. Some people around the area ran to catch me. *Hmm*, I later thought to myself, *what if the car had burst into flames or if the tree had not stopped the car, possibly we would have drowned in the stream; or what if I had run into an on-coming vehicle?* I pondered all these and concluded that God had a purpose for saving me.

While we were standing by the roadside trying to figure out how we would get to Abeokuta, a good Samaritan stopped by and took us in his car to Abeokuta. My parents were very grateful to him.

At school, I joined the Scripture Union and

some of my friends were in Students Christian Mission (SCM), but without really understanding the meaning of being born again. Many of us attended their meetings then, more for the squash drink and sandwiches that were served. The first time I heard the phrase *born again*, it was from my father; and I asked the innocent question like Nicodemus asks in John 3:1-8, '. . . Nicodemus said to Him, "How can a man be born when he is old? Can he enter a second time into his mother's womb and be born?" . . .'

It was while I was doing my A Levels at Comprehensive High School, Ayetoro (COMPRO) that I first had a personal encounter with the Lord. My roommate, Tola Soleye, was born again and she ministered to me. At first reaction was, *what is new?* Afterall, I am from a Christian home. But one Sunday morning during the service ministration by Brother Bankole Olowoofoyeku, I was deeply touched. I answered the altar call and became born again.

At church, I was a Lady Helper, a member of Girls' Purity Band and of the Girls Guide. At the University of Ibadan, I attended the Bible Fellowship at Professor Aboaba's house regularly. After graduation, in addition to attending Sunday services, I attended Bible class at Shepherd Hill Baptist Church at Obanikoro, Lagos, under the pastorate of Rev. Adegbite of blessed memory. I also attended Friendship Bible Coffees with Mrs. Adenike Lesi of blessed memory and some others. It was rotated from house to house. It was at such fellowship in Mr. & Mrs. Alison Ayida's house that my friend, Nike Ladapo, and I first met Pastor Adejare Adeboye of

The Redeemed Christian Church of God (RCCG) in 1984. I remember he based his sermon that day on Psalm 23. Nike and I were at Law School then and were both attending St Saviour's Church, Race Course, Lagos. It was a small church at that time with a white pastor.

Somehow, I felt inadequate in my Christian life. I wanted to know the Lord more and grow in Him as admonished in 2 Peter 3: 17-18: "You therefore, beloved, since you know this beforehand, beware lest you also fall from your own steadfastness, being led away with the error of the wicked; but grow in the grace and knowledge of our Lord and Saviour Jesus Christ. To Him be the glory both now and forever. Amen."

Through the encouragement of my sister, Mrs. Folake Ogutuga, I joined the Full Gospel Businessmen's Fellowship, Ikeja Chapter, and I re-dedicated my life to Christ. Coming to know the Lord Jesus Christ and accepting Him as my Lord and Personal Saviour is the best thing that has ever happened to me.

After I got married, I joined the Ladies Christian Fellowship International (LACFI) through Martha Asehon fondly called Wangi, in 1990. There I became, to the glory of God, the first chapter leader of Surulere Chapter and also the National Assistant Secretary General of LACFI. I also attended the Bible College from where I received a certificate in Christian ministry.

At church, I joined the Cathedral Friendly

Society (Female wing) of The African Church Arch Cathedral (Bethel) of 59, Broad Street, Lagos. I also became a member of the Young Women Christian Association (YWCA) and a Lady Helper. I co-ordinated The African Church Evangelical Fellowship (TACEF) Cathedral Branch. To God be the Glory! I also co-ordinated the first House Fellowship Bible Study Centre of The Arch Cathedral which holds till date at Engineer & Mrs Sete Aiyede's residence in Gbagada, Lagos.

I was nominated and appointed the Legal Adviser of Ijesa Diocese of The African Church and Matron of Jehovah Nissi African Church Choir, Ilesa.

The Scripture says, '"The Spirit of the Lord GOD is upon Me, because the LORD has anointed Me to preach good tidings to the poor; He has sent Me to heal the broken hearted, to proclaim liberty to the captives, and the opening of the prison to those who are bound; to proclaim the acceptable year of the LORD, and the day of vengeance of our God; to comfort all who mourn, to console those who mourn in Zion, to give them beauty for ashes, the oil of joy for mourning, the garment of praise for the spirit of heaviness; that they may be called trees of righteousness, the planting of the LORD, that He may be glorified"' (Isaiah 61:1-3).

Inspired by these words, I was led to set up a fellowship for widows; five years after my late husband, Babatunde Ibironke SAN passed on. I agreed in the spirit with Pastor Bimbo Josiah Ajayi and Mrs. Grace Monye, both of RCCG (City of Palms) formerly known as Strait Gate parish, to start the

fellowship. Thus **Comforter's Companions Fellowship**, for the widows, the separated, the needy and those incarcerated, was birthed in November 2008. To God be the glory! In the same parish, I became a worker in April, 2010 and later Sunday School Teacher.

I believe very much in interdenominationalism because I know that our Lord Jesus Christ does not belong to any particular denomination, rather He says in John 13: 34-35, "A new commandment I give to you, that you love one another; as I have loved you, that you also love one another. By this all will know that you are My disciples, if you have love for one another." Though I belong to a local assembly, I worship and serve anywhere as led by the Spirit; to the extent that I was privileged to teach Sunday School both at RCCG and The African Church at the same period. I was appointed the first Secretary and was the only female member of Anglican-African Church Ecumenical Commission, Nigeria, for five years.

To God be the glory, year 2010 became a turning point in my Christian ministry. Although I had been privileged to minister in LACFI and a few churches before then, doors of ministrations opened to me in some other churches and conventions including TACEF London Convention and Christ House Bible Church in Manchester.

WORK EXPERIENCE

In 1980 and 1981, I took up vacation jobs as a clerical officer at Federal Ministry of Works and Surveys and

Assistant Executive Officer at Federal Ministry of Housing and Environment respectively through the encouragement and support of my aunt, Mrs. Abeni Oduntan, of blessed memory.

After being called to the bar, I did my primary assignment of the National Youth Service Corps scheme at New Nigeria Development Company (NNDC), Kaduna.

After youth service, I had a stint with a law firm, Clifford Smith & Co. before practising as a solicitor with Tola Odulaja & Co. for about two years. Thereafter, I was employed at Nigerian Bank for Commerce and Industry (NBCI) as Assistant Legal Officer. I resigned in 1990 to set up my chambers, Adebisi Ibironke & Co. and part-manage Biato Book Centre.

In 1998, my father offered me retainership in his Company, ORI'RE Company Ltd., a property management company where I served as General Manager and later became Managing Director alongside my legal practice. I thank God for giving me the strength, courage and wisdom with which I worked successfully through the years.

14

Chapter Three

HOW IT ALL BEGAN

The dream of many a young lady is to meet a God-fearing man to spend the rest of her life with, and to be happily married. My first boyfriend and I went out for about four years. Our family members knew one another, more so that we attended the same church at that time. Later on, I realised he was not ready for a serious relationship, I was hurt and heartbroken. The relationship went

15

sour. One day, while I was still at the University, I received a postcard from him after his graduation from the University of Ife (as it was then called) informing me that he had travelled abroad for further studies. I felt bad, thinking to myself that he did not tell me or look out for me before he travelled. That was the end of that relationship—no address, no phone number, no letters, no phone calls.

Another relationship went awry; and by the time I graduated from the university, I made up my mind not to go into any relationship for a while. That was still my position when I was at the Law School. I did not have any serious relationship; most of my friends were in relationships while I was usually alone most weekends.

I came to realise that for a happy marriage, it is better to seek the face of God and be patient. God is the giver of life and the One who instituted marriage. He alone sees and knows the hearts of men. Jeremiah 17:7-10 says, "Blessed is the man who trusts in the LORD, and whose hope is the LORD. For he shall be like a tree planted by the waters, which spreads out its roots by the river, and will not fear when heat comes; but its leaf will be green, and will not be anxious in the year of drought, nor will cease from yielding fruit. The heart is deceitful above all things, and desperately wicked; who can know it? I, the LORD, search the heart, I test the mind, even to give every man according to his ways, according to the fruit of his doings."

With this understanding, I put my trust in God

for a life-partner, not to choose by myself anymore but to allow God to lead me.

* * *

At the Law school, I was a member of the Students Representative Council. Twice I attended meetings chaired by the then director of the school, Mr. Babatunde Ibironke. He was not yet a Senior Advocate of Nigeria at that time. He taught us Professional Ethics and Criminal Procedure. During the school year, he lost his wife and many of us students attended the burial. I was not close to him in any way, neither did he even know my name until the last day of school. I just knew him as my lecturer and director of the school,

After our final exams, we had a students/staff cocktail party which was the usual practice at the Law School. At the cocktail party, students move about to interact with their lecturers and invited judges. That evening, I was in the company of my friends, Nike Adeoye (now Mrs. Ladapo) and Uyi Emovon.

While walking around, we met the director, Mr Babatunde Ibironke, Late Justice Ayorinde, and Mr. Lanre Onadeko who was also a lecturer at the school then. He later became the Director General of the school. We all exchanged pleasantries and introduced ourselves. That was the first time that the director got to know my name.

Nike was living with Mrs. Hairat Balogun, the then Attorney General of Lagos State. I used to spend a lot of time with her. We studied together being on the same Adeola Odeku Street in Victoria Island, Lagos, where I also resided at the NTA staff quarters granted me by our family friends, Mr. and Mrs. Ade Okubajo. Uyi too was staying in a room within the same quarters.

When we returned to the quarters after the cocktail, Uyi said to me in pidgin English, "Director gree your own o." I asked her why she said so, she said she noticed the look in his eyes, I just laughed and forgot about it.

The year at the Nigerian Law School passed and I was posted to Kaduna for my National Youth Service Corps (NYSC) scheme. It is a program made compulsory for all graduates of tertiary institutions in Nigeria to enable the youth to know other parts of the country apart from their state of origin or town. It also serves the purpose of learning the culture and language of other regions in Nigeria and mixing with the people.

One day while I was meditating, I heard the voice that I would be Mr. Ibironke's wife. I resisted the voice because he was quite older than me and I knew my parents would not agree to that.

I came home from Kaduna for Christmas holiday and I needed to collect my transcript from the Law school. When I got to the administrative block, I met Mr. Ibironke. To my surprise he remembered my name and asked me how my service year at Kaduna was going. We exchanged contact numbers and I left.

Back in Kaduna after the Christmas holidays, I received a phone call at the office from him—there were no mobile phones then. He invited me to come

and see him when next I was in Lagos. I met him on my next trip and almost from the onset, he expressed interest in a serious relationship. Of course, I told him that it was not possible and that my parents would not agree to such a relationship, especially my father, who was a disciplinarian.

Babatunde Ibironke looked at me and said, "A Christian may say that it is not going to be easy but never that it is impossible." He went on to say that I should keep an open mind and commit it to God in prayers. What he said lingered on in my mind. To be honest, I liked him but I was not thinking of marriage. I saw in him a respectable gentleman who had a loving home and whom my future husband and I could look up to for advice. In fact, when he first mentioned marriage, I proposed to him that I would introduce one aunty who I really liked and adored to him. But he insisted it was me he wanted.

I shared the whole issue with my eldest sister, Mrs. Funmilola Onanuga. Mr Ibironke was attending The African Church Cathedral Bethel (now Arch Cathedral) while I was attending The African Bethlehem Church at Ebute Metta, which was my parents' church.

My sister encouraged me to pray and fast about it, which I did. The issue was not just about the age difference; he already had many children and I was a young lady. It became a burden in my heart. One day, while I was having my quiet time with Jesus, I was led to read Joshua 1:1-9: 'After the death of Moses the servant of the LORD, it came to pass that the LORD spoke to Joshua the son of Nun, Moses' assistant, saying: "Moses My servant is dead. Now therefore, arise, go over this Jordan, you and all this people, to the land which I am giving to them—the children of Israel. Every place that the sole of your foot will tread upon I have given you, as I said to Moses. From the wilderness and this Lebanon as far as the great river, the River Euphrates, all the land of the Hittites, and to the Great Sea toward the going down of the sun, shall be your territory. No man shall be able to stand before you all the days of your life; as I was with Moses, so I will be with you. I will not leave you nor forsake you. Be strong and of good courage, for to this people you shall divide as an inheritance the land which I swore to their fathers to give them. Only be strong and very courageous, that you may observe to do according to all the law which Moses My servant commanded you; do not turn from it to the right hand or to the left, that you may prosper wherever you go. This Book of the Law shall not depart from your mouth, but you shall meditate in it day and night, that you may observe to do according to all that is written in it. For then you will make your way prosperous, and then you will have good success. Have I not commanded you? Be strong and of good courage; do not be afraid, nor be dismayed, for the LORD your God is with you wherever you go."'

After the fasting and prayer session, Mr. Ibironke proposed again and I told him that I was going to ask for a sign like that of Gideon in Judges 6: 36-40: So Gideon said to God, "If You will save Israel by my hand as You have said—look, I shall put a

fleece of wool on the threshing floor; if there is dew on the fleece only, and it is dry on all the ground, then I shall know that You will save Israel by my hand, as You have said." And it was so. When he rose early the next morning and squeezed the fleece together, he wrung the dew out of the fleece, a bowlful of water. Then Gideon said to God, "Do not be angry with me, but let me speak just once more: Let me test, I pray, just once more with the fleece; let it now be dry only on the fleece, but on all the ground let there be dew." And God did so that night. It was dry on the fleece only, but there was dew on all the ground.'

I said if I told my parents about him, especially my father, and if he didn't raise any objection, then I would know for sure that he was my ordained life partner. For quite some time, I was a bit confused and was almost sure my dad was going to refuse.

One day, I summed up courage and went to inform my father about him. My father was silent for a while, then he asked that we should both pray about it. After praying together that day, he asked me to invite Mr. Ibironke to come and see him. He came with his friends, Dr. Adewunmi Majekodunmi and Mr. Vincent Kukoyi now of blessed memory. My parents gave us their blessings. Although my mum was still a bit worried, Mr. Ibironke promised to take good care of me. That was how our relationship started.

Chapter Four

THE UNION

Rest assured that God had ordained this union, Mr. Ibironke and I got married after four years of courtship. It was a small ceremony at the Registry with relations from both families and very few friends in attendance. This was followed by the Yoruba traditional marriage ceremony the weekend after. My cousin, Yemisi Akinloye (now Mrs. Olaofe) was the chief bride's maid while Dr. Adewunmi

Majekodunmi was the best man.

Now it was not an easy task to be married to a man with many children, a live-in mother in law and some relatives. However, the Holy Spirit guided me and endowed me with divine wisdom; and took me through the school of patience to pull through.

Babatunde Ibironke (hereafter referred to as Mr. I) was a very loving husband and wonderful caring father to all our children. He was quite supportive and understanding. He believed so much in me, that he even authorised me to open his letters.

Our coming together drew Mr. I closer to God as he himself testified publicly on some occasions that our union reinvigorated his faith in God.

We had family evening prayers when we preached and prayed alternately. Sometimes, we involved the children in the preaching aspect. Our watchword was: a family that prays together stays together. I attended vigils every month in church. On a few occasions he accompanied me; and when he didn't, he was always there at the door to welcome me home at dawn. We both attended house fellowship at the home of Professor and Mrs. G.A. Olawoyin SAN.

After a few years together, we decided to complete a bigger house that we started earlier on but was disrupted because there was a rival claimant to the land. We wanted everyone to be comfortable. We had to make a lot of sacrifices and deny ourselves many good things to ensure the house was completed. Along the line, we had some financial constraints and Mr. I almost gave up on completing the house. I told him not to lose hope but we should

continue to put our trust in God, that He who began the building of the house shall complete it for us. This I said standing on the word of God to Zerubbabel in Zechariah 4: 8-9: Moreover the word of the LORD came to me, saying: "The hands of Zerubbabel have laid the foundation of this temple; His hands shall also finish it. Then you will know that the LORD of hosts has sent Me to you."'

It is always good to stand on the promises of God as found in the Scriptures. God surprised us in so many unexpected ways. A tenant whose rent was not yet due came up to pay two years rent in advance. A supply contract for law books was awarded to us, and an oil company in which we had an investment decided to sell to another company and they gave us the option to divest our shares. All these put together helped us to complete the house and we happily moved to our new home which some referred to as "mansion". In many circumstances, I exhibited faith to the extent that Mr. I branded me "an incurable optimist".

Our home was full of love, joy and unity despite having children from different mothers. We sang, danced, laughed and did lots of lovely things together—not by power, nor by might but by the Spirit. To God alone be all the glory. He fondly called me Mrs. I. or Darling or Auntie. Rarely did he call me by my name.

I remember that a lot of people including some of our family and friends were sceptical of the success of our union. They thought it would not turn out well, probably because of the age difference and the many step children; but God took absolute control and it worked out well to the praise of His glory.

Recently, I went to pick some roses from our garden, forgetting that even roses have thorns. As I was cutting them, the thorns tore into my fingers. Truly, marriage or life itself is not a bed of roses. There were challenges and periods of misunderstanding. When Joshua was to succeed Moses to lead the children of Israel, he asked God for help and God gave him the response that He referred me to when I was getting into this marriage, Joshua 1:5-9: '"No man shall be able to stand before you all the days of your life; as I was with Moses, so I will be with you. I will not leave you nor forsake you. Be strong and of good courage, for to this people you shall divide as an inheritance the land which I swore to their fathers to give them. Only be strong and very courageous, that you may observe to do according to all the law which Moses My servant commanded you; do not turn from it to the right hand or to the left, that you may prosper wherever you go. This Book of the Law shall not depart from your mouth, but you shall meditate in it day and night, that you may observe to do according to all that is written in it. For then you will make your way prosperous, and then you will have good success. Have I not commanded you? Be strong and of good courage; do not be afraid, nor be dismayed, for the LORD your God is with you wherever you go."'

In every challenging situation, I turned to God in prayers and drew strength from His word. He

helped me all the way, prompting me on the way to go and on the things to do and say.

I give all thanks, honour, adoration to our Lord God Almighty, our Saviour Jesus Christ, the Holy Spirit, our Guardian, Comforter and Great Teacher, having blessed me with a happy home.

Chapter Five

THE BITTER PILL

And so it happened that my children and I set out for the United States of America on vacation on July 29, 2003; first to Dallas, then to Minnesota, with New York and Maryland in prospect.

While in Minnesota with Auntie Deola Idowu (nee Soyomokun) and her family, I received a call from Mr. I that he was not feeling well, but it was not anything to worry about. This was a man who had always enjoyed good health. He had even gone abroad for a health check earlier in the year. After I received his call, Aunt Deola and I prayed for divine healing for him. I then informed the children that we would be returning home earlier than scheduled. I called the airline to change our return date. We were expected to pay a charge of $450 but we met with God's favour at the airport and it was reduced to $200.

We arrived on Friday, 22nd August, 2003. Mr. I was at the airport to welcome us. Two days after, we all went to Ilesa in Osun State of Nigeria being his hometown on 24th August, 2003 and worshipped at the church there. On Monday 25th August, he said he would like to see some doctors at Obafemi Awolowo University Teaching Hospital (OAUTH), Ile –Ife. We went there and they carried out some tests and scans, and also booked him for another test at the University College Hospital (UCH), Ibadan, on Wednesday.

On Tuesday 26th August, we took the children to Ikogosi warm springs at Ekiti. Little did we know that would be the last picnic we would have with Mr. I. He played and sang funny songs with the kids.

After the test at UCH on Wednesday 27th August, we returned to Lagos to normal life. We went back to OAUTH on Monday, 8th of September, on medical appointment after which we both went to Ilesa to sleep at our country home which was not far from Ife. The 9th of September, 2003 was our last time together in Ilesa.

On Friday 19th of September, we were preparing

30

to go to Ilesa but Mr. I came back a bit late from office, so we postponed the journey till the next day. Thank God we did. That Friday night around 1a.m., he complained of stomach ache, nausea and weakness. We had to rush him to Ikeja Medical Centre around 3:30am on Saturday, 20th September. He was moved to St Nicholas Hospital later that day.

We were there for about three weeks and few days; it was there that he was diagnosed with cancer. I was devastated. Nonetheless, I still had hope that he would make it. We joined hands several times to pray and he exhibited faith. He was always singing the song "Heal me hands of Jesus." Very few of our friends who knew he was admitted in the hospital came to visit him. One of our family doctors with whom he was quite close, Dr. Babatunde Dinyo was in the United States at that time, but he called and spoke with him almost every day. There was a day that both of them broke down in tears on the phone.

I had to suspend my work and put some of my clients' briefs on hold. I remember I got a call from one of my corporate clients concerning a particular document, and when he heard that I was in the hospital with my husband, he offered to get the document drafted by their in-house legal officer. It was brought to me for vetting and signature and I was paid immediately after. That was God at work, our Great Provider.

There were days Mr. I felt a bit better. Unfortunately, one of the essential drugs for his management became scarce in Nigeria. Two close relatives living abroad, Mrs. Titi Esho and Tolu

31

Soyomokun swung into action and did their best to send the medicine. I remember that the day we received the medicine, Mr. I stood up from the bed and danced with gratitude to God, but that was short-lived. His condition became worse, but I still had hope that he would get well. At a point my faith failed when I saw Mr. I's health ebbing away, but I refused to accept that he was close to death. Whenever I broke down crying, he too cried and said he hated to see me cry. Time and again I ran to the bathroom to cry, pleading with God in prayers to heal him.

While we were at the hospital, I was concerned for our youngest son, Oluwafakinkunmi who was just ten years old at the time. Whenever he came back from school, he was alone most of the time until his older siblings came back from work. I did not like that at all so I arranged for him to move in with Tutu, one of his married sisters. Our youngest daughter, Oluwafeyikunmi who was twelve years old at the time was in the boarding school in Ibadan. She knew that her dad was not feeling well but I could not bear it to let her know the severity of the illness.

A year before then, when her dad and I visited her during one of the visiting days, we met with the Chief Executive Officer of the school, Mrs Lillian Bademosi. She invited Mr. I to be the chairman at the 5th Anniversary of the school and gave him a year notice. We all laughed and said that was such a long notice, not knowing that Mr. I would be in the hospital when the anniversary day finally came. I had to go to Ibadan with two of our sons, Jimi and Jide to

represent him. I quickly prepared a speech to deliver on his behalf and had to put up a brave face that all was well; especially because of our young daughter who did not even know that her dad was admitted in the hospital.

When we arrived at the school, I could see the disappointment in her face when she did not see her dad with us. I told her that the doctor advised him to rest. The event went well. My speech was greatly applauded even beyond my expectation. Thereafter, I was invited to meet the CEO in her office, and since I was alone with her, I told her the truth. Being a devoted Christian herself, I urged her to pray along with us. While speaking with her, I broke down in tears and had to clean my eyes so my daughter would not notice the agony within me.

October 11 was another visiting day. I went with her older sister, Taiwo, and her younger brother to visit her. We called her dad on phone and she spoke with him. Our daughter noticed that her dad spoke with difficulty. I observed the tears in her eyes and tried to comfort her, telling her that all would be well. As young as she was then, she took it upon herself to fast and pray for her dad's divine healing. But it was not to be. That was the last day she spoke with him.

Mr. I was discharged on October 14, 2003. At home, we employed two nurses from MFM healing and hospital ministry, Nurses Bunmi and Vicky; they were very caring. Two of the older children who were already married, Patricia whom we fondly call Lady P and Fidelimma, were with us throughout at the hospital and even at home. Till the last moment, we had vigils together. Mr. I branded us *The Three Musketeers.*

All the children are wonderful; they really cared for their dad. They showered him with love and appreciation and paid over fifty percent of the hospital bill. Adetutu and Taiwo took turns in taking care of their youngest brother, Oluwafakinkunmi, in their homes while I was in the hospital with their dad.

The evening before he passed on, Professor Afolabi Lesi and his wife, Professor Funmi Lesi, who is Mr. I's niece came home to examine him. They called me and our daughter, Taiwo, who is also a medical doctor aside, and said it was a hopeless case. I was shattered. I called the boarding school to check on our young daughter, but she could not speak to her dad because he was sleeping at the time. A lot of things were happening at the same time. He started having pains. I was dismayed; and just as Jesus said at the garden of Gethsemane, the night before He was crucified, "'If it be Thy will, let this cup be removed from me, yet not my will but Thy will be done'" (Luke 22:42), I surrendered to God and prayed that His will be done.

My darling husband, Babatunde Abiodun Ibironke SAN breathed his last on Sunday, 19th October, 2003 at around 2am; the very day that his church society, Cathedral Friendly Society (CFS) of which he was the President of the Male wing, had their anniversary in church. That night, five of us were with him in the room, the two nurses, Lady P, Fidelimma and me. I was with him on the bed. We

were both watching Billy Graham's evangelical outreach on TBN channel on the television. Surprisingly, we all dozed off about the same time for few minutes. He put his hands in mine and when I suddenly woke up, I noticed that his neck had tilted. The nurses tried to take his blood pressure but could not. Alas, he was gone! It was hard to accept. I felt betrayed.

I thought about my daughter and my concern was to quickly bring her home to break the news to her; before the dailies published it—since her dad was a public figure. Thanks to my brother in law, Mr Babatunde Ogutuga, who drove all the way to bring our daughter home. It was not easy breaking the news to my young children at their tender ages.

It was very kind of Mrs. Mosun Olamilokun to have helped in taking Oluwafeyikunmi back to school and for bringing me food. I cannot but remember Rt. Rev. Olu Akiode (now of blessed memory), the then Bishop of Lagos Diocese of The African Church, for his advice and encouragement. He told me that whenever they were holding any meeting anywhere to which I was not invited, I should pray that the Spirit of Jesus, the omnipotent, omniscient and omnipresent God, who is present everywhere at the same time, should enter such meetings on my behalf. My dear friend, Yemi Ogedengbe, also said the only prayer she was praying for me was to have divine wisdom to know what to say and what to do at every step of the situation. Those prayer points were very useful and God proved Himself strong on my behalf.

Babatunde was laid in state at the Nigerian Law School on Thursday, 13th of November, 2003, where many eminent people paid tributes to him. Commendation service was held the day after at the African Church Cathedral Bethel, Lagos; after which a motorcade convoy took him to Ilesa for Christian wake. On Saturday, the 15th day of November 2003, we had a funeral service at Jehovah Nissi African Church, Ilesa, after which he was buried. That memorable day was also the birthday of the twin boys, Olujimi and Babajide. It was unsavoury for them to bury their dad on their birthday, but that was the date available in church.

During the burial, as the body was being lowered into the grave, our last born, Oluwafakinkunmi, who was just ten years old at the time said to me with tears in his eyes, "Mummy, that is not Daddy, that is just his body, Daddy is with Jesus." Somehow I believed that the Holy Spirit, the Great Comforter spoke those words of comfort through him at that darkest moment.

The Lord gave Babatunde to me on 15th February, 1986. We courted for four years and got married on 25th January, 1990. We enjoyed a blissful marriage blessed with very good children. On Sunday, 19th October 2003, the Lord took him home. Blessed be the name of God forever!

Chapter Six

AFTERMATH

The die was cast. I had to reorganise, manage the big home combined with work and business. It was tough to realise that what two people used to do had suddenly become one person's responsibility. But thanks be to God, He never let me go it alone.

There was so much to do in ensuring that the

young children were healthy, comfortable and successful in school. All the children cooperated with me. To God be the glory, there was no rancour nor conflict as to property issues. In fact, they all rallied round me as much as they could. The children continue to shower me with gifts. Abimbola, the eldest who they fondly call 'olori ebi,' meaning family head, bought me lace fabrics yearly; same with Kehinde and others. Olatunde, the eldest son, now of blessed memory, stood in for his dad to play a father's role to his younger siblings.

Lady P stayed further with me for a while even after the burial whilst Fidelimma paid me frequent visits. She brought a group called "Women of Faith", who cares for widows, to have fellowship with me. Segun was always ready to accompany me to functions. Adetutu, Taiwo, Kehinde, Jimi and Jide were always checking on us even after they all got married. They paid us frequent visits with their families. Damilola too, though young, doted on her siblings from time to time.

As usual in the Nigerian culture, many people came visiting. Tolu Soyomokun came all the way from England for his uncle's funeral and spent few days with us. I quite appreciate Ebenezer Olamilokun, my late husband's nephew, as well as his wife, Ronke, for the role he has been playing in the family both before and after his uncle's death.

I thank God for all my siblings and their spouses, for surrounding me with much love and care; most especially His Grace, The Most Rev. Abraham Onadotun Onanuga, who was then the

Primate of The African Church, and his wife, Mrs. Olufunmilola Onanuga, my eldest sister. I bless God for my dear friends turned sisters, Mrs. Folasade Adetiba of blessed memory, Mrs. Anike Agbeja and Mrs. Ruth Idris for their prayers and unflinching support before, during and after the burial. In fact, Mrs. Idris left her family for about three weeks to stay with me. She has always been giving me spiritual and emotional support. Only God can reward their labour of love.

I held on to the word of God in Isaiah 54:4-17: ' "Do not fear, for you will not be ashamed; neither be disgraced, for you will not be put to shame; for you will forget the shame of your youth, and will not remember the reproach of your widowhood anymore. For your Maker is your husband, The LORD of hosts is His name; and your Redeemer is the Holy One of Israel; He is called the God of the whole earth. For the LORD has called you like a woman forsaken and grieved in spirit, like a youthful wife when you were refused," says your God. "For a mere moment I have forsaken you, but with great mercies I will gather you. With a little wrath I hid My face from you for a moment; but with everlasting kindness I will have mercy on you.... For the mountains may depart and the hills be removed, but My kindness shall not depart from you, nor shall My covenant of peace be removed," says the LORD, who has mercy on you. "O you afflicted one, tossed with tempest, and not comforted, behold, I will lay your stones with colourful gems, and lay your foundations with sapphires. I will make your pinnacles of rubies, your gates of crystal, and all your walls of precious stones. All your children shall be taught by the LORD, and great shall be the peace of your children. In righteousness you shall be established; you shall be far from oppression, for you shall not fear; and from terror, for it shall not come near you. Indeed, they shall surely assemble, but not because of Me. Whoever assembles against you shall fall for your sake. "Behold, I have created the blacksmith who blows the coals in the fire, who brings forth an instrument for his work; and I have created the spoiler to destroy. No weapon formed against you shall prosper, and every tongue which rises against you in judgment you shall condemn. This is the heritage of the servants of the LORD, and their righteousness is from Me," says the LORD.'

I kept reminding God that He was now my Husband and Father to my children, because He is the Husband of widows and the Father of the fatherless. God proved Himself in many ways.

Despite all the people that came to support, there were moments that I found myself alone in the house. A friend of mine who was widowed earlier had warned me that there would be such times of loneliness.

On a certain day I went to the market to buy some foodstuffs. As I was passing in front of a stall where I used to buy the kind of meat that Mr. I preferred, the seller recognised me and said, "Are you not buying meat for your husband?" I felt a sharp pain in my heart when I told the seller he had passed on.

I started receiving prayers and encouraging text messages from some people. The first of such messages came from Venerable A. A. Odufuwa, now an archbishop. Forwarded messages were not common then as we now have it on social media. Those messages usually came at the right time when I was downcast. Representatives of TACEF came home several times to have fellowship with me. Mrs. Adejuyigbe from another fellowship also called and sent messages frequently to check on us.

My mother passed on two months after my late husband. It was another blow to me, though she had suffered stroke for some years. As I told a friend of mine, I felt as if the compact disc of my life was fast forwarded, but the Great Comforter comforted me. I was very close to my mum. The joy of the Lord was my strength and I was not put to shame.

Nike Ladapo was always calling from Dallas to encourage me and pray with me. She sent me Bibles of different versions, journals and inspiring books. I received books written by some widows from my sister, Folake, and her husband, Uncle Tunde Ogutuga.

We had to move to a smaller house, not only because it was not easy to maintain a big house, but it was also the plan between Mr. I and me that when all our children are married, we would move to a smaller house. It happened earlier than expected. I personally had never really liked a big house; for me it was a relief, but not so for my children. Leaving the house where they spent most of their childhood years and saying bye to neighbourhood friends was a bitter pill to swallow.

I did my best to renovate the small house and make it as comfortable as possible. In no time, the children, though sentimental, became understanding and supportive of the decision to move to the new house. I remember them telling me that the big house without their dad was not the same. We had to partition and renovate the former house to get it rented out. That took a lot of my time coupled with some administrative issues like probate, but God helped me all through.

"Trust in the Lord with all thine heart and lean not on your own understanding; in all your ways acknowledge Him and He will make straight your paths" (Proverbs 3:5-6). I made it habitual to commit everything to God in prayers and His presence is ever with me and my children. There were times that the children took ill, but the healing stripes of Jesus healed them. There was even a time that my son was attacked, only God saved him and I am eternally grateful to God for sparing his life.

In my grief, there was a time I was angry at God, asking, 'Why?' But when I thought of it, I quickly prostrated and asked for forgiveness. Who am I to question God? There were worse cases around me, so I repented and the Lord strengthened me.

My son came to meet me one day with a sad face and asked me why we had not been going out as often as we did when their dad was around. I looked at him and tears started rolling down my cheeks. He put his face on my bosom and cried even louder. I sat him down and explained that mum was now busier than

before, and I tried to reassure him as best I could.

The first Christmas season without Mr. I was drab, coupled with the fact that my mum passed on a week to Christmas. At first, I did not feel like decorating the house, but then I realised that my children were grieving the loss of their dad too, and it would be so unfair to deny them what they were always looking forward to. They enjoyed mounting the Christmas tree. At a point, the Spirit rebuked me for grieving like those who had no hope.

There was a day that I was just drinking Fanta, something that I was not doing before. My daughter looked at me surprisingly and asked me why I was taking the fizzy drink. I told her it was just because I was feeling sad. She felt for me.

At times, I got easily irritated, and took it out on my poor children. When people like my siblings and nieces visited me to spend few days with me, my spirit was lifted; but no sooner had they left than I began to feel lonely again. So, each time they came, I felt as if they were drawing me back on my emotional healing process, but they did not know. They just couldn't. Only people who have had my kind of experience know how it feels; and even then, we take it differently. I remember that one of my in-laws who lost his wife some years earlier told me that he felt the same way when people visited him after he lost his wife.

I woke up one day and asked, "Lord why am I so lonely?" I found myself discussing with my children what was too much for them to comprehend at their tender ages.

I should not forget to mention that the two school directors of my children's schools paid us a visit—Mrs. Bimbo Fisayo of CTC International School, and Mrs. Lilian Bademosi of Christ Ambassadors International School (CAIC), Ibadan, who came with her husband, Dr. Yele Bademosi of blessed memory. CAIC gave my daughter scholarship for a school term that year. That was very thoughtful of them. I thank God for them.

Raising children alone was not an easy task, especially through their teenage years. I always stand on the word of God in Isaiah 54: 13 that my children shall be taught of God and great shall be their peace. God helped me in various ways to admonish and guide them. Whenever they wanted to go out and it did not agree with my spirit, I just turned to God in prayers. Without them knowing that I had prayed, they would come soon afterwards to tell me they had shelved their plans. It was either they lost interest in going or their friends did not come to pick them. God Almighty is indeed with us.

To the glory of God, both Oluwafeyikunmi and Oluwafakinkunmi did excellently well in their studies and graduated with first class honours from their respective universities. At their convocation ceremonies and on all such occasions, I wished their dad was there to see our kids grown and academically successful; which had been his dream for them.

There were many occasions in which God gave us victory. Let me share two of them.

On 1st of March, 2006, a room at the boys'

quarters of our home caught fire due to an electrical fault, but God in His infinite mercies sent help and the fire was put out.

In April of the same year, a bullet entered my office through the roof and landed on my desk. If I was in the office at that time, it could have landed on my head, but glory be to God, I was not there.

Chapter Seven

COPING WITH WIDOWHOOD

Widowhood is a bitter pill. I do not pray it for anyone, particularly young women, neither do I pray widowerhood for young men. Some people lapse into depression because in some cases, people who are expected to support them actually make life very difficult for them; especially in some cultures in Africa. People forget that at one time or the other, we all are going to leave this world.

In my own case, to God be the glory, a lot of people came around to commiserate—family, friends, neighbours, colleagues, fellowship and church members. All my children including step children surrounded me with love. There were many people praying for me even without me knowing. I only discovered that later. People sent me biblical messages that came in just at the right time in different situations.

All these came to be not by my power, nor by my might but by the Spirit of God, the Great Comforter. God kept His promises to me through Jesus Christ as I held on to His word in Isaiah chapter 54 quoted earlier.

At this point, let me share with you some steps to take in coping with widowhood:

1. First and foremost, you need Jesus Christ in your life. If you have not accepted Him as your Lord and personal Saviour, now is the time to get close to Him and have a personal relationship with Him. He alone can comfort you through the Holy Spirit.

Family and friends might despise and forsake you, but Jesus will never leave you nor forsake you. He knows you in and out and knows your situation. He feels what you feel and empathises with you. Hebrews 4:14-16: "Seeing then that we have a Great High Priest who has passed through the heavens, Jesus the Son of

God, let us hold fast our confession. For we do not have a High Priest who cannot sympathize with our weaknesses, but was in all points tempted as we are, yet without sin. Let us therefore come boldly to the throne of grace, that we may obtain mercy and find grace to help in time of need."

2. Search the Scriptures. I have always been a lover of Scriptures and one of the first things that I did after I was widowed was to check through a Bible concordance and highlight passages pertaining to widows and the fatherless. God cares specially for widows, orphans, the fatherless, strangers, the oppressed and the broken hearted. You will find comfort as you study and meditate on His word. Here are a few passages to encourage you--

Psalm 68:5: "A Father of the fatherless, a Defender of widows, is God in His holy habitation."

Psalm 34: 18: "The Lord is near to the broken hearted and saves those who are crushed in spirit" (NIV).

Psalm 30:5: 'For His anger is but for a moment, His favour is for life; weeping may endure for a night, but joy comes in the morning.'

Exodus 22:22-24: '"You shall not afflict any widow or fatherless child. If you afflict them in any way, and they cry at all to Me, I will surely hear their cry; and My wrath will become hot,

and I will kill you with the sword; your wives shall be widows, and your children fatherless."'
James 1:27: "Pure and undefiled religion before God and the Father is this: to visit orphans and widows in their trouble, and to keep oneself unspotted from the world."
Jeremiah 49:11: "Leave your fatherless children, I will preserve them alive; And let your widows trust in Me."

3. Join a Christian Fellowship, especially for widows. You will meet other people in similar situations or even worse situations than yours, to share your experiences, to pray together and to encourage one another. Before we started Comforter's Companions Fellowship, the first widows fellowship that I discovered was at CLAM (Christ Living Spring Apostolic Ministry), co-ordinated then by Pastor Mrs. Adegunwa, now of blessed memory. I also received newsletters from Fellowship of Christian Young Widows and Widowers by Lisa Lanussi and they were quite helpful.

4. Pray without ceasing (1Thes 5: 17). You need to pray for yourself, for your children and intercede even for those who you do not know. One may be wondering, how do you pray when something bad has just happened? Some of us even ask 'why'? The truth is that Jesus did not promise us a hitch free life but whatever we

go through in this life, He is there with us. In fact, He says in John 16:33: "These things I have spoken to you, that in Me you may have peace. In the world you will have tribulation; but be of good cheer, I have overcome the world." And the word of God says in Isaiah 43:2, '"When you pass through the waters, I will be with you; and through the rivers, they shall not overflow you. When you walk through the fire, you shall not be burned, nor shall the flame scorch you."'

Prayer is very essential. You might face reproach in widowhood whereby some people would want to take advantage of you. I usually reminded myself that our Lord Jesus Christ was reproached and insulted for our sake.

Let me share two instances amongst others, where the devil wanted me to be in fear but God gave me victory through prayers.

The first case was when my son was still in junior secondary school. I received an anonymous text message on my phone saying that I should not reply the text nor call the phone number, but I should send some money in a certain form or else my son was no longer safe. I just lifted that text message to God in prayers, since He is the Defender of widows and the Father of the fatherless. That night the Holy Spirit ministered to me that I should hold my peace and nothing would happen to my son. To God be the glory, I did not send any money and God protected us and still does.

The second case was when I received an anonymous phone call. The caller said some people sent him to execute me and my children, but he did not want to do it, and that was why he called to negotiate with me. He then hung up the phone. I did not say any of these to my children because they were still young then and I did not want them to live in fear.

I immediately handed the matter to God in prayers to overturn the devices of the evil one. God says in Isaiah 65: 24, '"It shall come to pass; that before they call, I will answer; and while they are still speaking, I will hear."' The Spirit ministered to me and gave me courage. He said that if the caller called again, I should rebuke him in the name of Jesus. Lo and behold, the assassin called again, while he was still trying to threaten me, I just rebuked him with a loud voice in the name of Jesus Christ and he never called again. Glory be to God.

Prayer is a two-way communication that entails worship, supplication, intercession and thanksgiving. When we pray, we are strengthened; and it is good to wait and be silent because God wants to speak with us too. This is how you get divine guidance and direction. God does speak to us in other ways.

He speaks through the Scriptures, through dreams, through His true messengers, through situations and circumstances, and sometimes directly to your heart through the promptings of The Holy Spirit.

5. Do not make any rash decisions. Take each day as it comes so you do not make mistakes.

6. Surround yourself with mature Christians, friends with positive thinking and attitude; people who will help you grow spiritually.

7. Loneliness is a major challenge in widowhood. You suddenly find yourself without your spouse. One terrible thing about loneliness is that you may be in the midst of people and still feel lonely. That actually happened to me, I felt seriously lonely even in the midst of people. Some people find solace in having a companion, but I just told myself I was not going to have a companion. Do not think that I am a superstar. No, I had sexual urge too at times because I am human. I did not want to be a second wife to any man or destroy another woman's happiness, so I prayed that if it was God's will for me to remarry, He should bring his ordained man for me, but if it was not His will for me to remarry, He should please give me the grace to remain single.

Admit your feelings and desires to God. Do not

deny it and do not live for pleasure, as admonished in 1Timothy 5:3-14, "Give proper recognition to those widows who are really in need. But if a widow has children or grandchildren, these should learn first of all to put their religion into practice by caring for their own family and so repaying their parents and grandparents, for this is pleasing to God. The widow who is really in need and left all alone puts her hope in God and continues night and day to pray and to ask God for help. But the widow who lives for pleasure is dead even while she lives. Give the people these instructions, so that no one may be open to blame. Anyone who does not provide for their relatives, and especially for their own household, has denied the faith and is worse than an unbeliever.

"No widow may be put on the list of widows unless she is over sixty, has been faithful to her husband, and is well known for her good deeds, such as bringing up children, showing hospitality, washing the feet of the Lord's people, helping those in trouble and devoting herself to all kinds of good deeds.
As for younger widows, do not put them on such a list. For when their sensual desires overcome their dedication to Christ, they want to marry. Thus they bring judgment on themselves, because they have broken their first pledge. Besides, they get into the habit of being

idle and going about from house to house. And not only do they become idlers, but also busybodies who talk nonsense, saying things they ought not to. So I counsel younger widows to marry, to have children, to manage their homes and to give the enemy no opportunity for slander" (NIV).

I also advise that you meditate on the book of Ruth. It really ministered to me that God has the power to restore.

8. Socialise, visit friends and family, try not to stay home alone where possible. Attend birthday and wedding celebrations, rejoice with those who rejoice and mourn with those who mourn. Attend a Bible-believing church where the true love of Christ is preached and practised. Keep yourself busy for the Lord. I kept myself very busy with church activities and non-governmental organisations.

You could also take up a course of study or vocation. Few months after I was widowed, I registered at Aptech for studies in Information Systems.

9. Take care of yourself and your children, they are your priority. Cast your burdens upon the Lord for He cares (see 2 Peter 5: 7). He is a Great Provider. He will sustain you (see Psalm 55:22).

I have heard from some widows, testimonies of how God showed up for them in their time of need. I also experienced that in many ways. In fact, there was a day that we did not have enough rice at home and I just told myself that I was not going to buy. It was Mr. I who used to buy bags of rice for the home. So I prayed to God that since He is the Husband of widows and Father to the fatherless, He should provide rice for us. Lo and behold, before the end of that week, my sister, two in-laws and a few other people brought us bags of rice without me asking anyone. It was a miracle to the extent that I started giving out rice to some less privileged people. Do not get yourself into unnecessary debt. Give to the needy if you can and encourage other widows. I had the privilege to visit and minister to some young widows in their homes and at Comforter's Companions Fellowship outreach.

10. Take your children out once in a while; watch good, inspiring movies and comedies, laugh your sorrow away, sing and listen to good music.

11. Read good books relevant to your situation. Let me mention a few books I read: *His Beauty for My Ashes* by Tai Ikomi, which she wrote after she lost her husband and three children in an accident; *Beauty for Ashes* by Joyce Meyers; *He*

Has Turned My Mourning into Dancing by Solape Mark-Obaba; *Life Without Limbs is Life Without Limits* by Nick Vujicic, which is about an inspiring man born without limbs; yet he surfs, skydives, swims and paints. He is an evangelist and motivational speaker helping those in depression. His condition notwithstanding, He is married with kids.

12. Learn to sing soul-lifting and comforting hymns and spiritual songs. There are some hymns that are popularly sung in churches today which were inspired and composed by men and women faced with trials. I will mention three out of them:

(i) *It Is Well with My Soul* written by Horatio Spafford, a prominent American lawyer and Presbyterian church elder. He composed the Christian hymn following a family tragedy in which his four daughters died aboard the S.S. Ville du Havre on a transatlantic voyage; the same year that he lost many of his business assets in Chicago fire. The first verse of the hymn is reproduced here:

When peace, like a river, attendeth my way,
When sorrows like sea billows roll;
Whatever my lot, Thou hast taught me to say,
It is well, it is well with my soul.

(Refrain:) It is well (it is well),
with my soul (with my soul),
It is well, it is well with my soul.

(ii) *What A Friend We Have in Jesus* by Joseph Scriven, composed after losing his fiancée the night before his wedding and following the news of his mother's illness. The lines are as below:

What a friend we have in Jesus,
All our sins and griefs to bear!
What a privilege to carry
Everything to God in prayer!

Oh, what peace we often forfeit,
Oh, what needless pain we bear,
All because we do not carry
Everything to God in prayer!

Have we trials and temptations?
Is there trouble anywhere?
We should never be discouraged—
Take it to the Lord in prayer.

Can we find a friend so faithful,
Who will all our sorrows share?
Jesus knows our every weakness;
Take it to the Lord in prayer.

Are we weak and heavy-laden,

Cumbered with a load of care?
Precious Saviour, still our refuge—
Take it to the Lord in prayer.

Do thy friends despise, forsake thee?
Take it to the Lord in prayer!
In His arms He'll take and shield thee,
Thou wilt find a solace there.

Blessed Saviour, Thou hast promised
Thou wilt all our burdens bear;
May we ever, Lord, be bringing
All to Thee in earnest prayer.

Soon in glory bright, unclouded,
There will be no need for prayer—
Rapture, praise, and endless worship
Will be our sweet portion there.

(iii) *Blessed Assurance, Jesus Is Mine* by Fanny Crosby; her real name, Francis Jane Crosby. She wrote more than 8,000 hymns, some of which are among the most popular in many Christian denominations. She wrote so many that she was forced to use pen names, lest the hymnals be filled with her name above all others. The most remarkable thing about her was that she composed those hymns in spite of her blindness which started six weeks after she was born due to a doctor's mistake.
Amongst her hymns are: *To God Be the Glory*

Great Things He Hath Done, Pass Me Not My Gentle Saviour and *Safe in the Arms of Jesus*.

I found comfort and encouragement in these hymns and many more. I hope this would go a long way in helping you.

And so it was, after about ten years in widowhood, I opened my Facebook page one day and I saw a friend request from my first boyfriend, Rotimi Awonuga, who I mentioned in Chapter Two of this book. At first, my reaction was friend request for what? This was someone who I had not seen nor heard from for over thirty years. The last correspondence was when I was at the university. I received a postcard from him telling me that he was in France for architectural studies—no phone number, no address. For over thirty years there was no communication between us. He then woke up one day and decided to find me on Facebook. I did not respond until after about three months. I just could not think of connecting back with him.

Meanwhile, I had been praying for a husband when I was convinced I needed to move on with my life. A year before then, at the first TACEF (The African Church Evangelical Fellowship) London Convention, held at Melia White House Hotel, my friend turned sister, Mrs. Folasade Adetiba (now of blessed memory) and I communed as we left the venue of the convention. We both said it would be good to come back to the place but not as singles. We held hands and prayed that we should be divinely connected to our rightful life partners, as long as it was God's will for us to remarry.

After I responded to Timi's friend request on Facebook, we started having telephone conversations, finding out about each other's lives all the while, what and what had happened in the last three decades.

One day, I was in England to visit my son and I received a call from him. He asked if he could come to meet me in England. *Why not?* Three days after, he arrived in Hatfield from France. While he entered the Galleria through the south entrance, I entered through the north entrance. We almost passed by each other. If I had not seen his picture on Facebook, I might not have recognised him. He had changed

more than I expected. He had lost his afro hair style but was still good looking. You can imagine the first meeting after over three decades.

Of course, he was very glad to see me and I was happy to see him too. He stayed in his hotel and I stayed in mine. We had dinner together and took a trip down memory lane. He tried to explain what led to our break up back then. We were both young and he wanted to explore the world. Anyway, he asked for forgiveness and I told him I'd forgiven him a long time ago. However, we didn't refresh our relationship. We both decided to be friends across the ocean.

The following year I visited France. I didn't stay with him. I stayed in a hotel. It was December and Christmas was in the air. He came over and took me out for dinner and sightseeing. I enjoyed my visit, but had to return to Nigeria before Christmas.

He called me on Christmas Day to wish me Merry Christmas and then, surprisingly, he asked for my hand in marriage. He said that he had been praying for a Christian wife and he believed God had answered his prayers. He went further to say he once missed the opportunity to get married to me and did not want to miss it again.

On my part, I needed to seek God's face if truly he was the one for me because I did not want to make a mistake. I continued to pray that God should reveal it to me if that was His will for me. Without discussing him with my friends, one of my Christian sisters, Mrs. Anike Agbeja, called me about two weeks after and told me about a dream she had indicating that I got married again. Few days after, I went to a hospital to see my friend turned sister, Mrs. Ruth Idris, whose daughter had just been delivered of a baby. As we were both walking out of the hospital, she suddenly asked me if I had been praying concerning remarriage and I said yes. She then smiled and said that while she was interceding for me during her personal devotion, she asked the Lord to bless me with another loving husband. She said the Lord replied her that He had already answered that prayer.

I thought to myself that what she said was the confirmation I needed, as the Scripture says that out of the mouth of two or three witnesses shall every word be established. I was then convinced that Timi was the one for me. That was how God removed my reproach. Being addressed as a widow usually refreshed the memory of my loss. I found it distasteful; my children too never liked me being called a widow.

The Psalmist says:
"I waited patiently for the LORD;
And He inclined to me,
And heard my cry.
He also brought me up out of a horrible pit,
Out of the miry clay,
And set my feet upon a rock,
And established my steps.
He has put a new song in my mouth—
Praise to our God;
Many will see it and fear,
And will trust in the LORD.

Blessed is that man who makes the LORD his trust,
And does not respect the proud, nor such as turn aside to lies.
Many, O LORD my God, are Your wonderful works
Which You have done;
And Your thoughts toward us
Cannot be recounted to You in order;
If I would declare and speak of them,
They are more than can be numbered" (Psalm 40: 1-5).

These words came to fulfilment in my life. Indeed, God, the Holy Spirit is the Great Comforter who saw me through. I pray that all widows and widowers who desire to remarry will divinely meet their rightful spouses in Jesus name.

Chapter Nine

RESTORED ON A MISSION ABROAD

At every stage of our relationship, Timi and I kept our children posted. Some of my children had always been praying and wishing that I remarry because they hated to see me sad and lonely, more so that they all have their lives to live. They were very happy and excited when we announced to them that we would be getting married.

Some of my friends and relatives had also been advising me to remarry. Worthy of mention is Mrs Eden Okoro whose husband is a minister in our church. She calls me "Queen" and came up to me several times to say that she had been praying for me to have a "king" because she did not like seeing me alone. In fact, one day after service, she came to me and said, "If only you can marry my husband." I burst out laughing, I knew she did not really mean it, but it was just an expression of love and deep concern for me.

To God be the glory, we got married in October 2015, twelve years after widowhood. Some of our children, siblings and few friends were in attendance at the wedding.

Some of our friends who knew us when we first met back then were happily amazed. They said, "At last, it took about forty years from your first meeting for you both to be married."

Three months after our wedding, I relocated to France with mixed feelings; leaving my family and friends especially my daughter. Although she wanted me to get married first, I wanted her to get married before me. Thank God she is now married.

Imagine coming to France in my mid-fifties, not being able to speak or understand French. It was tough initially for I couldn't express myself among people and friends in the community. I could not practise as a solicitor because of the language barrier. I had to change my vocation to teaching. I teach English language as a foreign language both to adults and

children. I attended French Language classes. I also attended International TEFL Institute in Paris. To God be the glory, I now speak French at intermediate fluency and enjoy my career as an English Teacher.

Another area of challenge was having to go through a driving school. I did driving tests both oral and practical, to be able to drive in France. Anyone who is familiar with the French driving licence procedure would confirm that it was like crossing a big bridge to have passed the tests. The Great Comforter was ahead of me at every step of the way and He is ever present with us.

I am blessed with more step children by reason of the second marriage and they are also very good, affectionate children; Toki, Toye, Eniola and Shadé.

My husband, Oluwarotimi Awonuga is a very loving husband, understanding and humble. He tries his best to make me happy and accepts all my children and family with love. He is my historian on world events whose watchword is "Above all else, love."

There were times that it was very necessary for me to be with my children who are now living in different parts of the world, but I could not, mostly because I had to wait for a visa. What I did in such situation was to pray and commit them as usual into God's hands; and our omnipotent, omniscient and omnipresent Father has always been with them.

I keep standing on His word in Isaiah 54:13, that my children shall be taught of the Lord and great shall be their peace. Even when I am with them, I cannot protect them, neither can I protect myself. God in His infinite mercies is indeed the Father to the fatherless.

Isaiah 41:10 is also another passage that I hold on to and it says, "Fear not, for I am your God, be not dismayed, for I am with you. I will help you and uphold you with the right hand of my righteousness."

I believe strongly that my mission in France is not just about marriage but to impact lives with the love of Christ. I pray that many who are yet to know Him will come to His saving knowledge and have a personal relationship with Him.

You might feel lonely but you are not alone; Jesus is with you. Surrender to Him, let Him into your heart. He will be with you, guide you and comfort you by His Holy Spirit, the Great Comforter.

Have you been deserted, disappointed or devastated in any way? Please do not contemplate suicide. God is love and He loves you much more than you can imagine. John 3:16: "For God so loved the world, that He gave His only begotten Son, that whoever believes in Him should not perish but have everlasting life." Grab the Scripture and start reading from the story of Jesus, the New Testament gospel. His words are spirit and life.

I pray that the Great Comforter will meet you at the point of your needs and comfort you in Jesus name. Remember that weeping may tarry for a night, but joy comes in the morning (see Psalm 30:5). Remember also that the Lord is near to the broken hearted and saves those who are crushed in spirit (see Psalm 34:18).

Chapter Ten
❖

WHEN THE WORLD STOOD STILL

It was in winter of December 2019, that a deadly virus broke out in China called coronavirus and renamed Covid-19. At first, many countries around the world thought it was just something that started in China and would end in China, but before long, it had spread across the globe hitting Europe and USA badly.

On March 11, 2020, the Director of World Health Organisation, Dr. Tedros Adhanom Ghebreyesus declared the Covid-19 a pandemic. By that time, some countries including Italy, France, Spain, United Kingdom, United States of America, Canada had started lockdown of schools, and before long, all these countries and many others including Nigeria, were on total lockdown.

Businesses were closed, churches, mosques and other places of worship were all locked down, gatherings were banned and weddings had to be postponed. Stay-at-home and social distancing orders were enforced in many countries.

There were travel restrictions across the globe, many airports were shut, airlines grounded their planes, world economies crashed, many people lost their jobs while some were on furlough.

Thousands of people including children were without food in some countries. By the end of May, over three hundred thousand people had died of the pandemic; including some health workers, doctors and nurses who risked their lives to save others.

Families were separated, people could not attend the burial of their loved ones. Hospitals were overfilled, isolation centres were set up to quarantine those infected, and some retired medical personnel were recalled. There were volunteers from other nations less affected, the lockdown was unprecedented in peace time.

On Good Friday and Easter Sunday, many churches resorted to online services and a few had a drive-through kind of service in which case members

stayed in their cars to listen to sermons. Face masks became the order of the day. It was a very sad period in history.

It was in the midst of this, that my daughter gave birth to my first biological grandchild in Canada. I could not travel to hold and cuddle him and give my daughter the necessary support because of the travel restrictions. I praise and thank God for granting my daughter safe delivery and for His constant presence with her and her family. He surrounded them with love. I appreciate the support of my school best friend, Olubola Okuboyejo and her family who reside in Canada.

My heart goes out to many families that have lost loved ones either to the Covid-19 pandemic or horrible happenings around the world, including terrorist attacks and wars.

I salute the courage of health workers all over the world for their sacrifice. I pray for divine healings for those who are sick and comfort for the bereaved.

As at the time of concluding the writing of this book, there was so much uncertainty in the world but I know the One who holds the future. He is Almighty God, the Alpha and Omega, the Beginning and the End, the Great Comforter. Only He knows the end from the beginning.

If you are yet to know Him, why don't you surrender to Him today and start a personal relationship with the Lord and Saviour Jesus Christ, who died that we may have eternal life. And though the world rolls by, there is hope for another life with

Him where there is no death, nor sickness, nor tears, nor sorrow; as written in Revelation 21:4: "And God will wipe away every tear from their eyes; there shall be no more death, nor sorrow, nor crying. There shall be no more pain, for the former things have passed away."